Snapshot Encounters

Brianna Poster

Copyright © 2011 Brianna Poster

All rights reserved.

ISBN: 1461054990
ISBN-13: 978-1461054993

DEDICATION

This book is dedicated to my grandfather, Floyd Ross. He was the greatest prayer warrior I have ever known; a passionate writer, musician, and wood carver; and one of my greatest sources of encouragement.

And to Sarah Buller, who taught me that life is too short not to take in every "Snapshot Encounter."

CONTENTS

Acknowledgments	1
Scripture Copyright	3
Message from Brianna	4
Why 40 Days?	5
Needing God	6
Approaching God	8
Power in God	10
God, Your Strength	12
Trusting Promises	14
Answered Prayer	16
Details of Scripture	18
The Mysterious God	20
Treasures of God	22
Your Soul	24
A Pure Heart	26
Empty Space	28
The Fatherless	30
Trust in the Rabbi	32
Being Held	34
Sheep and Shepherds	36
Following	38
Friend of God	40
Casting Your Cares	42
Living as a Victim	44
A Reason for All	46
The Low Points	48
Struggling Alone	50
Hope in Struggles	52
Desert Times	54

Sitting in Silence	56
Changing Thoughts	58
Heaven's Culture	60
Spirit and Flesh	62
Your Focus	64
Words and Actions	66
The Tongue	68
Absent-Mindedness	70
Being Alone	72
Your New Name	74
Your Purpose	76
Being Known	78
Being Remembered	80
Defying Criticism	82
Believing	84
Contact Info	86

ACKNOWLEDGMENTS

I would like to thank the following people for encouraging me to always press forward in my dreams:
Beka Hardt for believing in me, and in this devotional. I could not have done it without your constant support.
Courtney Anderson for writing my "about me" so I didn't have to write about myself in third person and for using her imaginative genius to help me with ideas for this book!
Har Lindgren for being the best "step grandpa" and promoting this book from his "favorite step granddaughter from Chicago!"
Mom for teaching me who God is and for and encouraging my growth in a relationship with God, whether He takes me across the state, across the country, or across the world!

All Scripture quotations are from *The New American Standard Bible* (NASB). Copyright 1960, 1962, 1963, 1968, 1971, 1972, 1975, 1977 by The Lockman Foundation.

Message from Brianna

God is always speaking, yet we so often miss out on His wisdom because of the chaos and noise in this world. This book captures glimpses of God that He has shown me, pieces of Himself that He reveals, and ways to see Him in the everyday. I desire that others understand and truly know these elementary truths that encompass the great love of our Father.

The title is specific, coming from a special encounter with the Creator. While I was driving past a beautiful scene of the vast ocean on one side, mountains in front of me, and the sunset to my back, I attempted to take a picture to capture some of the glory of the moment. Yet, no matter how much I tried, I could not fit even a portion of the beauty into the small frame of the camera.

We are much the same as that small picture. The Bible says we are created in the image of God (*Genesis 1:27*), however we are just a glimpse of who He is. No one on earth will ever come near to capturing the beauty, the splendor, and the glory of our living God. Each short devotion captures a small aspect of who God is; they are pieces of the puzzle into a better understanding of our marvelous God.

My prayer is that God would touch your life through what He has revealed to me, that the glimpses of Him in these short devotions will not be the only glimpses you see, but they will empower you to see God more every day and will come in contact with a very real God, the only real God, and that these encounters will mark your life for Him, forever!

Why 40 Days?

The number of probation or the act of testing, Biblically, 40 signifies the testing or trial of a person's character: Jesus was in the desert for 40 days, Noah and his family lived through the 40 days and nights of the flood, Israel was in the wilderness for 40 years. It additionally signifies a generation: many judges ruled for 40 years, and Saul, David, and Solomon each reigned as king for 40 years.

God chooses to use those times of trial and testing to refine our character. As we go through difficult times and situations, it is as though we are climbing a mountain; some days there are easy paths to follow, other days we have to scale the cliffs. But the best part of walking a mountain with God though, is that He is there to catch you if you fall.

This devotional is meant to draw you deeper into relation with God and to allow Him to work in you. It is for the generation who desires to seek after God's heart because, *"God is with the righteous generation"* (*Psalm 14:5* NASB).

I pray that as you seek God through these "snapshot encounters" that you will allow Him to refine you, as gold is refined through the fire and impurities are removed. I pray that my words will disappear and all you will read are words from your loving Father who cares so deeply about you.

"The Lord bless you and keep you; the Lord make His face shine upon you and be gracious to you; the Lord turn His face toward you and give you peace," (*Numbers 6:24-26*).

Focus On: Needing God

> "Religion that God our Father accepts as pure and faultless is this: to look after orphans and widows in their distress and to keep oneself from being polluted by the world."
>
> **James 1:27**

There is so much good you can do in this world, so much change you can bring, and a wonderful legacy you can leave. Yet, without Christ, the good, the change, and the legacy are empty. While religion is often seen as judgmental and law-based, God says it is so much more than that. His view of true religion is found in loving the unloved and serving the unserved while reflecting His light, instead of allowing darkness to impact your life.

Think about this: if poverty was brought to an end in an entire nation, yet Christ was not brought to those set free, they would still die malnourished because their spirits would not have been fed with Jesus, the Bread of Life *(John 6:35)*. To meet basic physical needs, yet leave an impoverished spirit does little more than extend a mortal life before an eternal destination. Without bringing God into the picture, your actions have only temporal meaning *(2 Corinthians 4:18)*. Your life must be marked by character of Christ. To make a difference, you must live differently.

"But the fruit of the Spirit is love, joy, peace, patience, kindness, goodness, faithfulness, gentleness, and self-control. Against such things there is no law. Those who belong to Christ have crucified the sinful nature with its passions and desires," (Galatians 5:22-23).

Your life needs to be characterized by the fruit of the Spirit, so when the world looks at you, they do not see you in the flesh but a reflection of God. You are called to change the world yet it is not an empty change, it is a change that revolves around the love God has for His children.

Exposure to: Needing God

1. What does "true religion look like for your own, personal life?

   _____
   _____
   _____
   _____

2. What fruits do you see in your life that is evidence of an absence of God's presence?

   _____
   _____
   _____
   _____

3. What fruits do you see that are an abundance of His presence?

   _____
   _____
   _____
   _____

Focus On: Approaching God

The description of the throne room of heaven is remarkable in both Revelation, as well as in Isaiah chapter six. Radiant jewels, thunder and lightning, unmistakable worship, a sea of glass, images that require absolute imagination to experience.

> **"Also before the throne there was what looked like a sea of glass, clear as crystal."**
>
> **Revelation 4:6**

So, imagine witnessing such a sight: being surrounded by the twenty-four elders, the winged creatures, and the sounds of praise. Imagine being on your face before this sea of glass and the throne of God where He is seated: to look up would mean to see God face-to-face, much like Peter facing Jesus as he asked to walk on the water. To look in Jesus' eyes means to trust Him enough to step forward into the unknown.

In the book of Matthew, Jesus spoke a single word to Peter, granting him the permission needed to approach the otherwise unapproachable, *"Come," (Matthew 14:29).* Though the throne room in Revelation is a much different story, still it is spoken, *"Come up here..." (Revelation 4:1).* God is granting you permission to approach Him and His throne of grace, to look into His eyes and see His splendor. Even when you are filled with fear and unbelief, God chooses to see the smallest bit of faith that you carry, and He allows you to walk on water, to approach what you cannot approach in your own strength.

You are God's child, and He is saying, *"Let the little children come to me, and do not hinder them, for the kingdom of heaven belongs to such as these," (Matthew 19:14).* More simply yet, He is asking you just to come, to sit at His feet and to witness who He is for yourself. All He desires is for you to know Him, and all else will flow from that intimacy.

<u>Exposure to:</u> **Approaching God**

1. How did you view yourself in the throne room of God? Hiding? Afraid? Joyful?

   _____
   _____
   _____
   _____

2. Is your view of intimacy with God one of fear or one of a son or daughter of the King?

   _____
   _____
   _____
   _____

3. Ask God how He views you. Wait for His response.

   _____
   _____
   _____
   _____

<u>Focus On:</u> Power in God

> "I can do everything through Him who gives me strength."
>
> **Philippians 4:13**

Have you ever spoken of what you cannot do in relation to your service for God? Whether using excuses or denying your abilities, it is so easy to shy away from serving. Often it is out of a fear that you are unable to be enough or do enough, yet it is true that, "God does not call the qualified, He qualifies the called," Author Unknown.

In your own strength, you are unable to make a difference for the kingdom of God. You need His strength to help you bring heaven to earth *(Matthew 6:10)*. If you refuse to allow Him to work based on your human reasoning, skill, or ability, then you are allowing lies to penetrate your thoughts instead of allowing God to prove His strength. If you are honest about what you are lacking, and use that as an excuse not to serve the Lord, then you open doors to give Satan the power that God deserves in your life.

God is all-powerful. Not only did He create the world, but He also created it to last through the years. Not only did He create you, but He also created your ability to have the freedom of thought. He allows you to go through what He knows you can handle. Though these times may be difficult, He will not leave you in need, nor will He leave you empty-handed. Instead, He will equip you to do all He has called you to during your time on earth.

"Now to Him who is able to do immeasurably more than all we ask or imagine, according to His power that is at work within us, to Him be glory in the church and in Christ Jesus..." (Ephesians 3:20-21). God's promises resonate throughout the Word. He is not a liar and does not promise what He will not fulfill. He is for you.

Exposure to: Power in God

1. What are some instances where you tried to make a change without God?

   _____
   _____
   _____
   _____

2. What has been a significant outcome of seeking God's desires for your dreams?

   _____
   _____
   _____
   _____

3. Ask God about one of your dreams. Why did He put it on your heart?

   _____
   _____
   _____
   _____

Focus On: God, Your Strength

> "Let us fix our eyes on Jesus, the author and perfecter of our faith…"
>
> **Hebrews 12:2**

It is so easy, in times of trial, to look inward at your struggles rather than upward to Christ. When you focus on yourself, you begin to dwell on your downfalls and shortcomings. And when everything else seems to be caving in around you, it only serves to magnify the problem. Often it is most difficult to seek God wholeheartedly in troubled times, yet those seasons have the ability to bring you to your knees in realization that God is your only hope in this dark world.

When you are *"hard-pressed on every side," (2 Corinthians 4:8)*, you must lift your eyes to the Lord remembering, *"[His] power is made perfect in weakness," (2 Corinthians 12:9)*. He promises that when you *"pass through the waters,"* He will be with you, and when you *"walk through the fire,"* you will not be overtaken *(Isaiah 43:2)*.

In life you will have times of rising waters and consuming fires, but if you allow God to shape your heart in those times, turning your eyes toward Him and not the world, He will mold you into something beautiful, just as diamonds are formed under the pressure.

"For you are a people holy to the Lord your God. The Lord your God has chosen you out of all the peoples on the face of the earth to be His people, His treasured possession," (Deuteronomy 7:6).

You undoubtedly will go through desert times where you feel lost ad the silence you encounter is deafening, yet when you face those times, you need to remember that God's response to "why" is that He knows the outcome of your life. It is for your benefit.

<u>Exposure to:</u> **God, Your Strength**

1. How have you grown closer to God in seasons of "floods" and "fires?"

   _____
   _____
   _____
   _____

2. What are some ways you connect with God in the fruitful seasons? Remember these in the barren seasons.

   _____
   _____
   _____
   _____

3. How can God show His power through your weakness?

   _____
   _____
   _____
   _____

Focus On: Trusting Promises

God and Satan are polar opposites. God is capable of only good, and Satan is capable of only evil. Therefore, God is not capable of lying because Satan is the father of lies *(John 8:44)*.

"**The promise us for you and your children and for all who are far off – for all whom the Lord our God will call.**"

Acts 2:39

Because God is incapable of lying, the promises He has given to you will be fulfilled. However, God works outside of time, so while He will fulfill His promises, your wait may be long, and you may not live to see your promises to completion.

God desires to give you the best in your life. Just like, for the Israelites, He desired to give the best of the land. He desires to bless you and see you through to your successes because He chose to allow Himself to be seen through you. Yet your vision of success may differ greatly from the Lord's. He has great plans for you, His precious child, but His full plan for your life may not be completely fulfilled until you join with Him in heaven.

God created the world and everything in it. When viewed in time, all of history plays out like one consecutive film to God, while to you, the span of your life alone is a film. So while God's plans go far beyond your life, and you are like an extra in the film, He relates to you as though you are the main character. His desire is that all of His children turn back to Him and find Him has He planned when He created the world. Your life and your legacy may live on well beyond your time on earth in order for God's plans to be completed.

'The Lord is not slow in keeping His promise, as some understand slowness. He is patient with you, not wanting anyone to perish, but everyone to come to repentance," (2 Peter 3:9). From God's patience in you, you can learn how to have patience for His promises. Because those promises are added blessings to life when your ultimate goal is to be in His arms.

<u>Exposure to:</u> **Trusting Promises**

1. What promises are you still waiting to have fulfilled?

   _____
   _____
   _____
   _____

2. What promises has God already fulfilled in your life?

   _____
   _____
   _____
   _____

3. Ask God for a new promise He has for your life.

   _____
   _____
   _____
   _____

Focus On: **Answered Prayer**

> **"Ask and it will be given to you; seek and you will find; knock and the door will be opened to you."**
>
> **Matthew 7:7**

In the church, prayer cards have begun to seem like nothing more than a kind gesture. Commonly, prayer is referred to as a last resort. Instead of the first option, it has become the last. Instead of desired, it has become forced. In this life, there are many distractions, from family to work, from games to the Internet, and everything in between. Instead of seeking God's heart, He is treated like a magical toy, only there when something can be gained from Him.

Maybe the correct treatment of God is lacking because faith in God and in the power of prayer is lacking. Or maybe the vastness of the world is seen and it is not understood as to how one person could have meaning to the Creator of it all. Our mindsets have become so fixed on this world, yet you are not a citizen here on earth but in heaven *(Philippians 3:20)*.

In Matthew chapter six, Jesus taught you how to pray. His words are as follows:

"...Your kingdom come, Your will be done on earth as it is in heaven," *(Matthew 6:10)*.

Prayers are not words reaching up to empty space, but they are emotions that flow to the heart of God. God has given you the ability to petition your requests to Him, and has said, *"Ask and you will receive..."* *(John 16:24)*. Prayer is not a required task but an attitude of the heart. And God promises that your prayers are not raised in vain.

Exposure to: Answered Prayer

1. When are some times God has answered your prayers?

   _____
   _____
   _____
   _____

2. When has God answered your prayers in a way that surprised you? Why was it unexpected?

   _____
   _____
   _____
   _____

3. Ask God if anything is distracting you from time in prayer with Him.

   _____
   _____
   _____
   _____

<u>Focus On:</u> Details of Scripture

The original Hebrew of the majority of the Old Testament has so much meaning and depth to it. A jot is the smallest letter of the alphabet. In Hebrews, the jot would be the "yod," which is like an apostrophe. Tittles were marks used in the rewriting of Scripture as checkpoints to confirm that the transferring was perfect. If there was a mistake in the rewriting, the entire page had to be rewritten by that scribe.

> "For assuredly, I say to you, till heaven and earth pass away, one jot or one tittle will by no means pass from the law till all is fulfilled."
>
> Matthew 5:18

Not only is the Bible very specific in the transferring of Scripture but also in the writing, because every letter of the Hebrew alphabet has meaning. For example, the Hebrew word for "fire" is "ash," which is composed of the letters aleph and shin. Aleph means "strength" and shin means, "to consume or destroy." So, when the letters of the word "fire" are combined, the meaning is "the strength to consume or destroy."

The Bible is much more than a collection of stories, it goes much deeper than is commonly realized. The words are more than words; they are descriptions of the world and of God. In John, it says that, *"in the beginning was the Word, and the Word was with God, and the Word was God." (John 1:1)*. The Word was God. It does not merely speak of Him it is He. Every detail of Scripture is a glimpse at the Creation.

Every detail has purpose, and every word proclaims the greatness of God. With even one of these words missing, Scripture would be incomplete just as a puzzle is incomplete without the final piece. And, in God's eyes, you are like that word or puzzle piece. Without you, the world would be incomplete.

<u>Exposure to:</u> Details of Scripture

1. What is something that, if missing from your life, makes you feel incomplete?

2. How do you best spend time with God to feel more complete?

3. Ask God to show you how integral you are to His plan.

Focus On: The Mysterious God

> "It is the glory of God to conceal a matter; to search out a matter is the glory of kings."
>
> **Proverbs 25:2**

The original Hebrew brings a depth to this verse that is otherwise not understood. Rewritten, this verse could say that the majesty, the splendor of our Lord is to keep hidden His inner workings; yet His divine authority allowing you to delve into His heart and seek out these secrets constitutes your soul. Part of what makes God glorious is that He hides certain truths, giving you the ability to seek Him out. As you seek out your Lord, you also seek out His heart and are drawn into what concerns Him that you may know Him more.

Deuteronomy 29:29 says, *"The secret things belong to the Lord our God, but the things revealed belong to us forever..."* The Word proclaims that God chooses to conceal certain matters, yet He equips those He has chosen to hear and be ruled by Him to seek out His heart and uncover these mysteries that His glory may be revealed.

The matters God chooses to hide and reveal are eternal. They are what He desires you to store up on as it says in Matthew, *"But store up for yourselves treasures in heaven, where moth and rust do not destroy, and where thieves do not break in and steal," (Matthew 6:20).* His treasures are eternal and cannot be taken from you.

The more you seek God, the more of His heart you will learn. As you enter into relationship with Him, your heart will be shaped and purified into a better reflection of your loving God. And the truths He reveals to you belong to you forever! *"Oh the depth of the riches of the wisdom and knowledge of God! How unsearchable His judgments, and His paths beyond tracing out!" (Romans 11:33).*

Exposure to: **The Mysterious God**

1. Write down some mysteries, or a revelation, that God has spoken to you.

2. What eternal treasures do you hold?

3. Ask God for a new revelation of His heart.

Focus On: Treasures of God

> "Then King Darius issued a decree, and search was made in the archives, where the treasures were stored in Babylon."
>
> Ezra 6:1

A king's glory is to search out what has been hidden *(Proverbs 25:2)*, but where has it been hidden? It has been hidden in the archives, the Word of God. If you read *Ezra 5:17*, you are told that the archives were also called the "treasure house." It was where the important articles were stored for safekeeping. If the archives were hidden in the "treasure house," then within the Word of God are the Lord's treasures.

Treasure. The word seems to mean so little anymore, yet it conjures up an image of wealth or riches that have been accumulated over time, things so precious and valuable. To God and His kingdom, the things of this world are not treasures, alternately, the Word says they will soon pass away and be destroyed *(Matthew 6:19)*. So why do Christians so often assume that God's blessings will come in the form of material possessions and wealth, which can only be received and utilized during your time on earth?

Though God does bless you in the physical, His treasures are things of eternal value. Such treasures are based on Him and His glory, on the everlasting Kingdom of Heaven. When you follow His Word, and when you seek His heart, then you will find true treasure!

"But seek first His kingdom and His righteousness, and all these things will be given to you as well," (Matthew 6:33).

When you seek God's treasure, it is as though you are diving into the sea of His love, and when you dig in to find His treasure, you must refuse to stop upon the first find and continue searching. This is God's desire for your life. The riches of God do not stop when you begin looking, but they become deeper as you dive in.

Exposure to: Treasures of God

1. What prevents you from digging deeper into God's treasure?

   _____
   _____
   _____
   _____

2. What are some physical things that have hindered your eternal pleasures?

   _____
   _____
   _____
   _____

3. Ask God for an opportunity to dive deeper into His love for you.

   _____
   _____
   _____
   _____

Focus On: Your Soul

> "What good is it for man to gain the whole world, yet forfeit his soul?"
>
> **Mark 8:36**

In this world, goals tend to be focused on success, popularity, leading, followers, reputation, and occupation. Yet those words coincide with a quote by William Pitt, which simply states, "Absolute power corrupts absolutely."

None of the aforementioned words are bad in their own right, but if you begin seeking them over God, they begin to change into something they were never meant to be. It is good to be successful in the sense of seeking after God's heart and persevering through failure, but when you seek success over His presence, you are no longer setting your sights on a good goal but are succumbing to this world.

If you were to gain all the money and power, fame and fortune of this world, and made it to the top then found out there was no God, would your life be any different? Are your sights being set on God and His desires for your life or focused on personal gain?

"Do not conform any longer to the pattern of this world, but be transformed by the renewing of your mind…" (Romans 12:2). In this world, the main priority tends to be similar to the American dream, freedom for the purpose of opportunity and success. Yet with God and the culture of heaven, your main priority should be to have your heart beating in time with the heart of God.

If your life could be lived in the same manner without God, why proclaim to follow Him? Thankfully, you serve a very real God who does exist. In your journey through life, it is important to keep your gaze fully fixed on Him, *"the author and perfecter of our faith," (Hebrews 12:2).* Live your life in a ay that is an outpouring to others of the in pouring of Christ to your heart.

Exposure to: Your Soul

1. What "*patterns of this world*" have you found yourself conforming to?

   _____
   _____
   _____
   _____

2. Define your view of success.

   _____
   _____
   _____
   _____

3. Ask God what His view of success looks like in your life.

   _____
   _____
   _____
   _____

Focus On: A Pure Heart

"Blessed are the pure in heart for they will see God."

Matthew 5:8

The meaning of purity has changed in recent years. In comparison to the past, it has become almost entirely disregarded. Clean, righteous, and holy are not words that would describe the majority of the population. In a world so defiled, how do you remain pure in heart?

Though your heart is an organ in your body, Scripture is not referring to the organ. The heart is referred to as the most important part of your body. It contains your thoughts and emotions. Holy and pure thoughts and emotions are what the Word is proclaiming you ought to strive after.

What you allow yourself to dwell on, what you value highly in your life, and how you feel about a situation determines the position of your heart. *Philippians 4:8* says, *"...whatever is true, whatever is noble, whatever is right, whatever is pure, whatever is lovely, whatever is admirable – if anything is excellent or praiseworthy – think about such things."* Accordingly, Matthew speaks of how even thoughts of sin would be sin in itself *(Matthew 5:27-28)*.

Keeping a pure heart is important for so many reasons. A pure heart will bring you closer to God and, *"out of the overflow of the heart the mouth speaks," (Matthew 12:34)*.

The focus of your heart is reflected in your words and actions. If your heart is pure, your words and actions will follow. Alternatively, if your focus is on the negative of a situation, your words and actions will also be negative.

The more you focus on living a pure life with a pure heart, the more you will be able to see God in the midst of the world.

Exposure to: A Pure Heart

1. Are you a "glass half empty" or a "glass half full" viewer? Why?

   _____
   _____
   _____
   _____

2. Are the majority of your thoughts about yourself positive or negative? Why?

   _____
   _____
   _____
   _____

3. Ask God how to begin working toward purifying your heart.

   _____
   _____
   _____
   _____

__Focus On:__ Empty Space

> "When [an evil spirit] arrives, it finds the house unoccupied... then it takes with it seven other spirits... and they go in and live there..."
>
> **Matthew 12:44-45**

God intentionally created your heart with a void in it. This void was created in every human since the beginning of time. Often, it has been attempted to be filled through the things that this world offers. The problem is that this void exists in your heart for a reason. It is a void created specifically to be filled with God, and nothing in this world will satisfy a life that is void of God.

If you fill your heart with that which is not of God, those things that you put into your heart are being reflected in your life. Once it has taken root in your life, it is difficult to remove that root. It is possible to remove the root, but it is often re-rooted with something else that is not of God.

Matthew 12:44-45 is also talking about your life. When you leave your heart devoid of God, even in a small area, you give the enemy a chance to come in and seize your heart in a more powerful way. It is as though you have set up a place that is comfortable for the enemy, not by pouring into him but by allowing him to gain footholds in your life.

The only way you can become whole is to live your life enraptured by the living God, not leaving room for anything that is not of Him in your heart. Your life needs to be consumed by the heart of God. Faith cannot just be something you profess; it must be something you live.

"Then they cried out to the Lord in their trouble, and He saved them from their distress. He sent forth His word and healed them; He rescued them from the grave," (Psalm 107:19-20).

Exposure to: Empty Space

1. In what ways do you try to fill the empty spaces in your life (ex. Video games, Internet, movies, etc)?

   _____
   _____
   _____
   _____

2. Has that given the enemy a foothold? In what way?

   _____
   _____
   _____
   _____

3. Ask God how to begin to fill your life with more of Him in place of distractions.

   _____
   _____
   _____
   _____

Focus On: The Fatherless

> "I will not leave you as orphans; I will come to you."
>
> **John 14:18**

It is so easy to become accustomed to ruled and conditional love. You may feel like a slave to the world, only considered a success when culture approves. However, God has a different view, on life and on you personally. His view is that you are loved, unconditionally. Regardless of where you are or where you have been, His love prevails and His *"mercy triumphs over judgment," (James 2:13)*.

You are loved. You are cared for. You are desired. You are delighted in. The Creator of the Universe made you, delicately and personally. He has chosen you to be His child, to know you intimately, to walk with you through life, and to guide you, *"for in [Him] the fatherless find compassion," (Hosea 14:3)*.

God is not distant; on the contrary, He desires to be a part of your daily life. He desires to be your Father, to raise you up in the same way His Son, Jesus, was raised from death. Humans are fallible. You will make mistakes that may cause others pain, and you will have mistakes made that cause you pain. Though God desires His children to be an example of Him and His love, *"all have sinned and fall short of the glory of God,"* (Romans 3:23). But those shortcomings do not change who God is.

Unfortunately, because humans are fallible, this world is full of broken people. So many have, or are, growing up without fathers, whether from abuse, absence, or otherwise just not present. But God desires that you know the perfect Father. While your earthly father may have failed, God is reaching out to you.

God loves you and has given you, *"...the Spirit of sonship. And by Him we cry, 'Abba, Father,'" (Romans 8:15)*. "Abba" means daddy, one of the first words a Hebrew child would speak. With open arms, you can reach out and fall into the arms of your true Father, God.

Exposure to: The Fatherless

1. What has life been like with your father? Was he a part of your life?

   _____
   _____
   _____
   _____

2. How has your view of your earthly father impacted your view of God, the Father?

   _____
   _____
   _____
   _____

3. Ask God to reveal Himself as the Father to you.

   _____
   _____
   _____
   _____

Focus On: Trust in the Rabbi

What would it take for you, as a modern day believer, to have faith in God like the disciples had in Jesus? Faith like theirs was a blind and Biblical faith. They would follow Christ wherever He went; not knowing exactly where He was leading, but knowing He would not lead them astray.

"We live by faith, not by sight."

2 Corinthians 5:7

A typical expression in the Jewish culture is to "be covered in the dust of the Rabbi". It was a great honor to follow a Rabbi; it meant that the person was of a chosen few. This phrase is understood to mean that the disciples would follow their Rabbi so closely that they would be covered in the dust from His sandals. They would walk with Him, follow where He went, and reflect His actions to the best of their ability. Their goal was to learn their Rabbi's yoke, His teaching, and then they would take that yoke upon themselves, teaching it to the next generation, their own disciples.

For so Christians, there is no longer the same outlook on following Christ. Instead of seeing it as an honor, it is treated as a burden. Instead of following closely behind Him and learning His ways, people try to choose their own path. But you serve a trustworthy and faithful God. He will not let you down or abandon you. So, why not choose to put your faith in Him and be covered in the dust of His sandals?

"Let us hold unswervingly to the hope we profess, for He who promised is faithful," (Hebrews 10:23).

To trust your Rabbi, Jesus, is not just to profess that you follow Him, it is to be able and willing to follow in His footsteps. The acts of love the Jesus performed and the life He lived are His yoke that you are to take upon yourself. It is not enough to profess with your lips if you do not follow with your life.

Exposure to: Trust in the Rabbi

1. What is your view of a Rabbi? Does that view look at all like how you view Jesus? Why or why not?

   _____
   _____
   _____
   _____

2. If your spiritual walk with Jesus was shown in the physical, would you be covered in the dust from His sandals?

   _____
   _____
   _____
   _____

3. Ask God to show you His yoke, His teachings.

   _____
   _____
   _____
   _____

<u>Focus On:</u> Being Held

> "Yet I am always with You, You hold me by my right hand."
>
> **Psalm 73:23**

How great a feeling it is to be held, to be safe, and to be secure. It is the feeling of being known and loved in the midst of an unknowing and often uncomforting world. So often, there is nothing more comforting than being in the arms of someone who loves you, who knows you deeply, and who cares for you.

However, being held by God presents a challenge, as He is not tangible but invisible. Though you, His child, exist to be His hands and feet for the world, there are many times when the ache to be held is so powerful and there is no one around who knows you. Being held by God is difficult to grasp yet surpasses being physically held by anyone in the world.

"Lay hold of My words with all your heart…" (Proverbs 4:4). You know that holding onto something does not need to be in the physical. You can hold to Scriptural truth and teachings in your mind, and you can hold promises in your heart until they come to pass. Being held by God is similar. When you take hold of His promises and allow them to become real to you, then you can feel the support of God as He fulfills His promises in your life.

"As I was with Moses, so I will be with you. I will never leave you nor forsake you," (Joshua 1:5). The difference in being held by God is that He is always present. It does not take a phone call to reach Him, you must simply cry out. After all, He is your Father. Your perfect, trustworthy Father.

Exposure to: Being Held

1. What is your greatest struggle in "holding on" to an intangible God?

   _____
   _____
   _____
   _____

2. Maybe it's not being held for you. What are other affirmations do you seek from people that should come from God?

   _____
   _____
   _____
   _____

3. Ask God to present Himself to you in that way.

   _____
   _____
   _____
   _____

<u>Focus On:</u> Sheep and Shepherds

"I am the good shepherd. The good shepherd lays down his life for the sheep."

John 10:11

Shepherds are constantly referenced in Scripture. Though they were often the lowliest in their families, the youngest son or weakest child, Jesus reaching out and connected Himself directly to them. Many time, it was the shepherds who saw the Lord. Maybe because they had fewer distractions than others, or maybe it was because God desires you to understand how much He cares for you despite what the world says about who you are.

A shepherd's goal is to care for his sheep. Shepherds would literally put their lives on the line for the sheep in their care, being the gates at night to keep them safe from predators. This was because sheep were the determinate of value in a family. They provided food, drink, and wool, and their horns were used to hold oil and to make musical instruments. The sheep needed to be cared for and tended to in order to provide for a family. In exchange, they would bring a good return for the family.

You are a lamb of God, and He is your Great Shepherd. He takes care of you, protects you, and lays down His life for you. In return, you are called to bring Him glory, for as He pours into your life; you are to pour back out into the lives of others.

Additionally, just as sheep know and trust the sound of their shepherd's voice, you should know your Shepherd so well that you can easily distinguish it from the voices of the world.

"...He calls His own sheep by name and leads them out," (John 10:3).

__Exposure to:__ Sheep and Shepherds

1. What do you feel your position is in your family or in life in general? Do you feel like the lowliest, the elect, or somewhere in between?

   _____
   _____
   _____
   _____

2. As sheep give a return of food, drink, and wool, what return can you give to this world?

   _____
   _____
   _____
   _____

3. You were created to hear God. Ask Him to teach you how to tune in to His voice.

   _____
   _____
   _____
   _____

Focus On: Following

Follow: to imitate or copy, to pursuit, to accept as a leader. Who and what you follow says a lot about who you are and the ideals that you hold.

> "At once they left their nets and followed Him."
>
> **Mark 1:18**

It seems as though the more this culture revolves around technology, the more people and things there are to follow. From those directly involved in your life, to bands and anyone in the spotlight, culture is fixed on this ideal of following someone. But are you as prone to drop everything and follow after Christ?

In Biblical times, the call to follow Christ was a call for the lowest in class to follow a Rabbi. Being under the direction of a Rabbi was the highest privilege in Biblical society. Jesus called after those who had not otherwise been allowed to learn from a Rabbi: fishermen, a tax collector, and a zealot. He chose those society considered to be the weakest.

Yet this culture is inclined to follow anyone and everyone. It is not understood that following someone, no matter how easy or difficult, always comes at a cost. By following closely to someone, you imply that you are in agreement with their standings in life.

Maybe there is a need to reevaluate who is followed and looked up to. Who are you, in a sense, endorsing? You are called to set an example of a righteous life for the world. Does who you follow match what you profess?

"...Set an example for the believers in speech, in life, in love, in faith, and in purity," (1 Timothy 4:12).

Exposure to: Following

1. Followers are marked by their ability to imitate that which they are following. How well do you imitate Jesus?

   _____
   _____
   _____
   _____

2. Who or what, if anyone or any trend, are you following where the ideals go against your profession of being a follower of Christ?

   _____
   _____
   _____
   _____

3. Ask God to shed light on anything keeping you from Him.

   _____
   _____
   _____
   _____

Focus On: Friend of God

Have you become friends with the world, choosing quick fixes and momentary pleasure instead of difficult processes that ultimately result in healing and eternal joy? Friendship with God is valued far above anything this world could ever provide. While there is good in the world, it is but a glimpse of the glory of God, and He desires you to stand apart from the world, not to conform to it!

"You adulterous people, don't you know that friendship with the world is hatred toward God? Anyone who chooses to be a friend of the world becomes an enemy of God."

James 4:4

Psalm 25:14 says, *"The Lord confides in those who fear Him; He makes His covenant known to them."* Only those who truly, deeply fear the Lord will He open up with. It is like a person sharing secrets with only those he or she is closest to. The Lord confides in, or shares the deep secrets of His heart, with those who fear Him. And you are given the authority to seek after those truths *(Proverbs 25:2)*.

What prize do you seek to obtain? Is it momentary, something that can be found in this world, or is it eternal, the hope you can hold to forever? Keep your eyes focused on the prize. Fear God and seek to love Him with your whole heart. It will be more beneficial than anything the world could ever offer.

"...And let us run with perseverance the race marked out for us," (Hebrews 12:1).

Exposure to: Friend of God

1. Do you desire to know the secrets of God's heart? Why or why not?

   _____
   _____
   _____
   _____

2. Often you may trust yourself less than God trusts you. Do you feel trustworthy to receive God's secrets?

   _____
   _____
   _____
   _____

3. Ask God to show you how to grow in trust with Him.

   _____
   _____
   _____
   _____

Focus On: Casting Your Cares

> "...Let us throw off everything that hinders and the sin that so easily entangles..."
>
> **Hebrews 12:1**

God never gives you more than you can handle, but you may take on too much. He chooses not overload you because He recognizes your need to lay everything at His feet, yet it is so easy to hold on to it and say, "Lord, here, You are my Master, You can have my life… but I'm just going to keep my hand on this." Or sometimes you have handed your life over to God, but when a piece of your world spins out of your control, you take hold of it all over again.

When times like this come, it is out of a lack of trust in God that you take back the control you had given to Him. The minute something is not going well, it is assumed that God does not have it under control, so you try to take over again.

But when did God lose His power to hold you in His hands? If you were to tell Him that you cannot hold on any longer, His response would be, "Why would you need to hold on when I already have you in My hands?"

As a human, it is easy to begin to lose sight of truth, to begin to think that the Creator cannot keep in order what He has created. But the truth is, He made everything and causes it all to work together for the good of His people *(Romans 8:28)*. Without Him, the world would fall apart completely, yet through Him, you are safe in His hands.

"He is before all things, and in Him all things hold together," (Colossians 1:17).

Exposure to: **Casting Your Cares**

1. How is it difficult for you to give God the control in your life?

   _____
   _____
   _____
   _____

2. Has there ever been a time when you feel God let you down?

   _____
   _____
   _____
   _____

3. Ask God where He was in some of your darkest moments.

   _____
   _____
   _____
   _____

Focus On: Living as a Victim

> "I will give you a new heart and put a new spirit in you; I will remove from you your heart of stone and give you a heart of flesh."
>
> **Ezekiel 36:26**

In life, you are faced with days when you can soar and days when you feel glued to the floor. Difficult circumstances have a way of keeping your feet on the ground and removing life from your spirit. So often, situations you have gone through are allowed to determine your future. They damage your thoughts and actions because they teach you to believe lies.

When you believe the lies, it seems logical to pick up a victim mentality and to begin to live as though everything will go wrong because so much already has. But this attitude is as damaging to others as it is to you. When you live as though everyone is against you, then you will tend to push everyone away, including God, the One who holds the Truth.

Believing the truth is difficult if you have grown up in lies. Even more difficult is belief in the supernatural truth that comes from God. Yet you are not of this world, your home is in heaven, and you were made for the supernatural workings of the Holy Spirit.

Though your spirit is worn down from the ways of this world, though your heart is broken and bruised, you still have the promises of healing from the Lord. No longer need do you need to live as a victim to your past, but you can now live in the freedom that is becoming a new creation in Christ. As *2 Corinthians 3:17* promises, *"...If anyone is in Christ, he is a new creation; the old has gone, the new has come!"*

God promises freedom in healing, and that freedom is for His glory. You can be fully restored through Christ Jesus!

"Then the nations around you that remain will know that I the Lord have rebuilt what was destroyed and have replanted what was desolate, I, the Lord, have spoken, and I will do it," (Ezekiel 36:36).

Exposure to: Living as a Victim

1. Do you, or have you, picked up a victim mentality? How has it affected you?

   _____
   _____
   _____
   _____

2. What are areas in your life that need restoration?

   _____
   _____
   _____
   _____

3. Ask God to show you some of the lies you believe about your life.

   _____
   _____
   _____
   _____

__Focus On:__ A Reason for All

To find joy in all circumstances, to rejoice in suffering, to go through trials, to be tempted; there is a reason for everything.

> "There is a time for everything, and a season for every activity under heaven."
>
> **Ecclesiastes 3:1**

God has plans for the weak and plans for the strong, for the prideful and for the humble, for the compassionate and for the weary. God has plans for all of His children, and He wants you to fight.

Throughout the book of Joshua it says, "*… be strong and courageous…*" *(Joshua 1:7)*. Joshua was facing a situation much bigger than himself. After Moses' death, God placed the leadership of Israel into Joshua's hands. In the midst of the new battle Joshua was about to embark on, God spoke to hum and asked him to fight.

Are you ready to give up? Then push through. Your trials are not setbacks, they are challenges. God is pushing and stretching you in order to grow you. Are you fighting the truth> Then turn to the Word. God will provide answers, but you need to seek them out. Are you struggling to find reason> Then look for the reason God created the world. Find love in the fact that God has a reason for your life. Do you struggle with love self-esteem? Focus your gaze on the King, the Creator of this world who made you, His masterpiece.

Maybe the answers are right in front of you. Maybe you have to dig deeper. Sometimes life can be all uphill while other times it is smooth sailing. But regardless of where life takes you, God is with you constantly. You need both winter and spring, both summer and fall. Each season of life is essential to living a full life in Christ. And you can find comfort knowing that you will never walk alone.

"*…The testing of your faith develops perseverance. Perseverance must finish its work so that you may be mature and complete, not lacking anything.*" *(James 1:3-4)*.

Exposure to: A Reason for All

1. What struggles are you facing right now?

   _____
   _____
   _____
   _____

2. What is your typical reaction to struggles? How does that need to change?

   _____
   _____
   _____
   _____

3. God has you in this season for a reason. Ask Him for a plan to make it through this season with strength.

   _____
   _____
   _____
   _____

Focus On: The Low Points

> "Therefore, I stationed some of the people behind the lowest points of the wall at the exposed places..."
>
> **Nehemiah 4:13**

Sometimes God chooses to place you in a position where you are not sheltered but exposed. This is not because He desires you to be hurt, but because He has brought you to a place where you are strong in the Him to be *"more than [a conqueror]," (Romans 8:37)*. When you have come to a place where you have the strength of the Lord, you are then able to fight on behalf of others in those situations.

In Nehemiah, chapter four, it continues on to say, *"...Fight for your brothers, your sons and your daughters, your wives and your homes," (Nehemiah 4:14)*. Often God will ask you to fight even though the battle may not be your own. He will place you in positions of risk because He has given you the strength to overcome in that situation. God's call for you is to reach out, *"...Encourage the timid, help the weak..." (1 Thessalonians 5:14)*.

When situations arise and you are called to fight for others, take hold of the truth and cover your life, your words, and your actions in the Word of the Lord. He has brought you to a place where you are able to stand firm in Him and intercede in the war for others. Allow God to move in you and through you, so that your actions, in His strength, will make a way for others.

"...We are weak in Him, yet by God's power we will live with Him to serve you." (2 Corinthians 13:4).

Exposure to: The Low Points

1. When has God asked you to fight a battle that was not a battle for your benefit?

   _____
   _____
   _____
   _____

2. Do you ever doubt your ability to be strong in positions the Lord has brought you into? Why or why not?

   _____
   _____
   _____
   _____

3. Ask God for the endurance to fight battles for others and to see the bigger picture in all circumstances.

   _____
   _____
   _____
   _____

__Focus On:__ Struggling Alone

> "...When [the devil] lies, he speaks his native language, for his is a liar and the father of lies."
>
> **John 8:44**

One of the devil's most powerful tactics is to tell you that you are alone when you most need community. At your weakest point, and in your deepest struggles, he tries to convince you that no one could possibly understand you or what you are going through. The truth is that we have all fallen short *(Romans 3:23)*, and there are areas in each of our lives where we have sinned.

In the midst of the devil's lies, you need to see the truth from God. He says, "*...Confess your sins to each other and pray for each other so that you may be healed," (James 5:16)*. Healing comes when you open up with what you feel you should hide. If you keep to yourself, it is almost as though you have an excuse to continue in your sins. But by allowing others into your life and opening up to them, you can be held accountable for your actions. And though accountability is difficult, God's promises always remain.

The prize you desire to reach is righteousness through Christ Jesus. Which is found in abundance where the presence of sin is absent. By allowing others into your life and revealing to them your struggles, you will continue on the path to righteousness and, *"The fruit of righteousness will be peace; the effect of righteousness will be quietness and confidence forever," (Isaiah 32:17)*.

Exposure to: Struggling Alone

1. When God created Adam, He said, *"it is not good for the man to be alone,"* (Genesis 2:18). Have you bought into the lie that you do not need people if you have God?

   _____
   _____
   _____
   _____

2. Do you have anything you have been struggling with in secret and need accountability in?

   _____
   _____
   _____
   _____

3. Ask God to show you some people who are safe to share your struggles with. Find time to meet with them about your struggles.

   _____
   _____
   _____
   _____

__Focus On:__ Hope in Struggles

"...I will make the Valley of Achor (Valley of Trouble) a door of hope."

Hosea 2:15

Sometimes, life can be a giant roller coaster ride. There are some seasons when you are on top of the world and can clearly see the promises God has for you, yet other times, you will be in the valley, with your stomach in knots, not knowing what will be coming around the next corner.

No matter what life brings your way, you are able to have hope in the Lord. He has given you the promise that where you have struggled, He will provide hope *(Hosea 2:15)*. You are also promises that, "*... in all things God works for the good of those who love Him, who have been called according to His purpose,"* *(Romans 8:28)*.

When you struggle, human nature is to focus on your shortcomings, but God desires you to look to Him instead. When you remember the hope that He has given to you as a gift, you will begin to see the sun rising on the other side of the valley. If your hope is in Christ and not in the world, you can be secure in knowing that God has your best intentions in mind because His plans for you are good *(Jeremiah 29:11)*. When you are seeking after God's heart, you will not fall but be guarded and protected within His path.

"*[You] have this hope as an anchor for the soul, firm and secure,"* *(Hebrews 6:19)*.

Exposure to: Hope in Struggles

1. In what ways have you lost hope in your life?

   _____
   _____
   _____
   _____

2. Have you been in, or are you in, a *"valley of Achor?"* How did you, or can you, find your way out?

   _____
   _____
   _____
   _____

3. Ask God what His plans are for you in this season.

   _____
   _____
   _____
   _____

Focus On: Desert Times

> "...I will lead her into the desert and speak tenderly to her."
>
> **Hosea 2:14**

During your life on earth, it is inevitable that you will face desert times; those dry times when God seems distant, everything around you is crashing down, and life seems barren. God will take you through desert times not to punish you but to show you His love. While that may seem backwards, it is during those times when you are dry and have nothing to offer that you realize your desperation for the only One that can supply your needs.

Jesus Himself spent time in the physical desert, relying on God's truth to make it through. He withstood temptation from the enemy and came out strong in the Truth to begin His ministry *(Matthew 4:1-11)*. Your times in the desert are not meant to wear you down. Instead, they cause you to seek God more, to dig deeper into His truth, and to help you find the spring of fresh water when you are surrounded by barren land. This produces a yearning to learn more about Him and uncover the secrets of His heart that He so desperately longs to reveal to you.

In those dry times, it is crucial that you do not give up fighting. You must continue to press into God and His Word in order to grow deeper in Him. As you do, He will trust you with more of His deep Truth. And when you uncover this Truth from God, you have but one thing to do with it: *"What I tell you in the dark, speak in the daylight; what is whispered in your ear, proclaim from the roofs," (Matthew 10:27).*

Exposure to: Desert Times

1. What is your greatest struggle in desert times?

   _____
   _____
   _____
   _____

2. How do you tap into God's renewal in your prosperous times? Record it below to remember for your dry seasons.

   _____
   _____
   _____
   _____

3. Ask God how He desires you to share His truth with the world around you.

   _____
   _____
   _____
   _____

__Focus On__: Sitting in Silence

"...After the fire came a gentle whisper."

1 Kings 19:12

There is so much noise in this world, so much to distract you from hearing God's voice with clarity and certainty. In a world where you are able to hear so much, from affirmations to criticism, you may greatly desire to hear the voice of God speaking audibly to you.

While God has the ability to verbally speak to you, He often chooses not to. As a believer, you need to learn to hear the sound of His voice, to learn the discipline of sitting in silence in order to hear His heart.

Even Jesus would withdraw from the crowds and find a place of solitude to meet with the Lord, *"But Jesus often withdrew to lonely places and prayed," (Luke 5:16).*

When was the last time you were in a quiet place: no voices speaking, no television static, phone turned off, and your heart quiet before the Lord?

There are so many things in this life to distract you from the voice of God; so much that speaks over His still, small voice. It's not that He desires to be in the background, but His desire is for you to seek after Him with all of your heart.

Imagine a friend is trying to talk to you from across a noisy room. Your friend's intention is not for you to struggle to hear what is being spoken but to share something that is meant for you and not the crowd surrounding you. In order to hear, you would have to escape the noise and draw nearer to your friend.

"But if from there you seek the Lord your God, you will find Him if you look for Him with all your heart and with all your soul," (Deuteronomy 4:29).

Exposure to: Sitting in Silence

1. What are some of the noises in your life (note: they may not all be physical noises)?

   _____
   _____
   _____
   _____

2. Have you heard God speak before? What did He sound like to you?

   _____
   _____
   _____
   _____

3. Ask God to speak to you, to reveal Himself to you, in a new way today.

   _____
   _____
   _____
   _____

__Focus On:__ **Changing Thoughts**

Have you ever hear someone say a word you know well, but they pronounce it differently than you would? Imagine their pronunciation was actually correct. In order to pronounce it correctly, you would need to completely relearn the word! There would be times when you would say it correctly, and other times when you would fall back into our original way of pronouncing it, yet we would learn through repeated practice.

"For we are God's workmanship, created in Christ Jesus to go good works, which God prepared in advance for us to do."

Ephesians 2:10

Your walk with God is very similar. You have grown up in a world where lies are more prevalent than the truth. So, changing thoughts that have flowed easily through your mind for years is no different than changing the way you would say a word. It takes time, it is a process, and you will not succeed on the first try. Yet, is there any reason to be discouraged? No! If you had the ability to change immediately, you would not need God.

Unless you stop on your journey, cease moving forward, and halt all progress, you have not failed and should not become discouraged. Not having it right just means you are imperfect, which is encouraging! Perfect people would not need God, they would be their own gods. For that reason alone, strive not to be perfect, but to love and follow God.

"...Love the Lord your God with all your heart and with all your soul and with all your strength and with all your mind..." (Luke 10:27).

Exposure to: Changing Thoughts

1. Are you a perfectionist? Does perfectionism limit or hinder your progress with God?

   _____
   _____
   _____
   _____

2. In what ways have you become discouraged in your walk with God?

   _____
   _____
   _____
   _____

3. Ask God for a boost of encouragement in your time spent with God.

   _____
   _____
   _____
   _____

Focus On: **Heaven's Culture**

> **"But our citizenship is in heaven..."**
>
> **Philippians 3:20**

This world is not your home or permanent dwelling. You are not called to be comfortable or satisfied with the culture of this world. You have your own cultures and traditions, a way of life that you are used to and, typically, comfortable with. However, when traveling in between cultures, the term "culture shock" is often used to define the difficulty acclimating between those cultures.

The Word says, *"Do not conform any longer to the patterns of this world..." (Romans 12:2).* Essentially, God, through Paul, is saying not to take on the culture of this world, because heaven is your home and final dwelling, not the world. To be surrounded by a culture and not be influenced by it is nearly impossible. However, you have the power of the Holy Spirit to influence and guide your steps in the culture of heaven. Therefore, you still have the ability to walk in step with your Lord, following His paths that He keeps straight for you.

The culture of heaven is unlike that of earth, and when you begin to walk in the culture of heaven, you will begin to see it come to earth. Additionally, you will be preparing your heart for your heavenly home.

"...We have a building from God, an eternal house in heaven..." (2 Corinthians 5:1).

Exposure to: Heaven's Culture

1. Have you ever experienced another culture? How difficult was it to acclimate between various cultures?

   _____
   _____
   _____
   _____

2. In your own words, what is the culture of heaven like?

   _____
   _____
   _____
   _____

3. Ask God to reveal to you new ways to live in the culture of heaven.

   _____
   _____
   _____
   _____

__Focus On:__ Spirit and Flesh

God's call to all believers is to bring heaven to earth and life to the dying. The way of this world is seemingly easy. Though life may be difficult, following the world is fun in the moment. Yet living in the world can wrap you up in such bondage. Though you may feel free, you are in chains, not answering the call of God.

"But small is the gate and narrow the road that leads to life, and only a few find it."

Matthew 7:14

Yet in *2 Corinthians 3:17* it states, *"Now the Lord is the Spirit, and where the Spirit of the Lord is, there is freedom."* Freedom comes from following the Lord and the ways of heaven, not from finding momentary pleasure in the world *(James 1:27)*.

You are called to bring Life by living in the Spirit. The road to Life is small and difficult, it presents obstacles and challenges, but the outcome is eternal. Living by the Spirit may be difficult, but it enables you to bring Life to those who encounter you. Because the Spirit resides in you, an encounter with you as a Spirit-filled believer is an encounter with the Spirit.

Though the call is difficult, you are to live by the Spirit, not the flesh. Still, the Word, which is alive and active, promises that, *"No discipline seems pleasant at the time, but painful. Later on, however, it produces a harvest of righteousness and peach for those who have been trained by it." (Hebrews 12:11)*.

Exposure to: Spirit and Flesh

1. How have you brought heaven to earth?

   _____
   _____
   _____
   _____

2. What does it look like to live by the Spirit rather than the flesh?

   _____
   _____
   _____
   _____

3. Ask God to help you to deny yourself *(Luke 9:23)* and live by the Spirit.

   _____
   _____
   _____
   _____

<u>Focus On:</u> Your Focus

> "**Let us fix our eyes on Jesus, the author and perfecter of our faith...**"
>
> **Hebrews 12:2**

Human nature is to focus on yourself. Especially in American culture, our minds tend to be focused only on our personal circumstances. Because of this, you can easily become depressed and overwhelmed by the world.

Imagine looking in a mirror, if you stare at yourself, your thoughts are focused on you. So continue to gaze and place your thoughts on Jesus. Picture Him seated on the throne in Heaven, at the right hand of God. When seeing and experiencing His might, His power, and His love; can you even see yourself anymore?

Whatever consumes your thoughts consumes your focus and whatever you are focused on determines how you view the world.

What reason, then, do you have to think of yourself when there is so much more to pour your time, energy, and attention into? Why wallow in guilt, shame, or self-pity when you can focus on the Lord?

Maybe who you are has nothing to do with you. Who you are is consistent with what motivates and drives you. Who you are is your heart and that revolves around the place that you fix your eyes.

"...Whatever is true, whatever is noble, whatever is right, whatever is pure, whatever is lovely, whatever is admirable – if anything is excellent or praiseworthy – think about such things," (Philippians 4:8).

Exposure to: Your Focus

1. How was it for you to look in a mirror while picturing Jesus?

   _____
   _____
   _____
   _____

2. How can you better "*fix [your] eyes on Jesus*" on a daily basis?

   _____
   _____
   _____
   _____

3. Ask God to help you to keep your gaze secure on Him.

   _____
   _____
   _____
   _____

Focus On: Words and Actions

How much of your life reflects that of Christ Jesus? Do you walk in step with the words that you speak? Is your life marked by the gospel? Do you stand out because of the way you live your life?

"...I beat my body and make it my slave so that after I have preached to others, I myself will not be disqualified for the prize."

1 Corinthians 9:27

Saying something is so much easier than actually following through with it, whether it be saying something easy like you will clean up your room or more difficult like proclaiming a walk with Christ. Claiming to be a Christian is much easier than living the life of a Christ follower. Yet, the Word says so much about the necessity of your actions matching your words.

"I know your deeds, that you are neither cold nor hot. I wish you were either one or the other!" (Revelation 3:15). You are not called to live an apathetic life but a life on fire through the Holy Spirit. The words you speak should be in line with the gospel, and the life you live should be consistent with both the gospel your words.

In Christ, you have been given new life with the ability to take off the old and put on the new. Because of this, that which before would consume you can be taken under the power of the Lord and contained so it will not have power over you anymore.

"...In all these things we are more than conquerors through Him who loves us," (Romans 8:37).

Exposure to: Words and Actions

1. Can you recall any times when your words and actions have not coincided?

   _____
   _____
   _____
   _____

2. How can you take care to line your words and actions up with the Word of God?

   _____
   _____
   _____
   _____

3. Ask God to show you where your words and actions have not been in alignment.

   _____
   _____
   _____
   _____

<u>Focus On:</u> The Tongue

Speech is a powerful tool in your life as a follower of Christ. In your words, you have the power to edify or the power to tear down. And, ironically, you have the power to do both simultaneously. In the book of James it says, *"Out of the same mouth come both praise and cursing…" (James 3:10)*. To curse is to speak harshly over someone, which is literally speaking death over his or her life. Your speech has the power to give life or to take it away.

> "…The tongue is a small part of the body, but it makes great boasts…"
>
> **James 3:5**

There are many people who grew up with only negative words being spoken over them. You never know the circumstances from which people are coming. The care with which you speak needs to extend beyond your own understanding and into the realm of unconditional love.

Not only do your words have an influence on others, but the words that you speak impact yourself as well. *"From the fruit of his mouth a man's stomach is filled; with the harvest from his lips he is satisfied," (Proverbs 18:21)*. If the words you speak carry life and death for others, they also carry life and death for you.

In order to have and to give a prosperous life, the fruit of your tongue must be good and pleasing to the Lord for, *"the tongue that brings healing is a tree of life," (Proverbs 15:4)*.

Exposure to: The Tongue

1. When have you used your tongue to bring death?

   _____
   _____
   _____
   _____

2. When have you used it to bring life?

   _____
   _____
   _____
   _____

3. Ask God how to control your tongue for the benefit of others as well as for yourself.

   _____
   _____
   _____
   _____

Focus On: Absent-Mindedness

> "And God raised us up with Christ and seated us with Him in the heavenly realms in Christ Jesus."
>
> Ephesians 2:6

Imagine being in the throne room of heaven. In fact, God declares you are seated there even now (*Ephesians 2:6*). Now, as you are seated next to God, imagine your life on earth. If you are living your life on earth oblivious to God, it is as though you are seated next to Him in heaven unaware of the happenings of heaven. Instead of taking in the power, glory, and majesty of your heavenly Father, it is as though you are sitting in heaven in a daze.

So often as Christians, we live like this. With the focus on the immediate, that which is seen and is presently important. But the Word says, *"God jealously longs for the Spirit that He made to live in us," (James 4:5)*. Not only are you seated in the throne room with God, but the Spirit of the Lord is dwelling within you. Therefore, whether you are absent-minded or fully focused, God desires the Spirit who resides in you. So, not only are you withholding yourself from God in those moments, but you are withholding Him from His Spirit as well.

Maybe that is why He desires you to be either hot or cold, to either have the Spirit or not (*Revelation 3:15*).

"But He gives us more grace," (James 4:6).

Exposure to: Absent-Mindedness

1. Do you fully take in the presence of God in your life?

   _____
   _____
   _____
   _____

2. How could you become more aware of His presence?

   _____
   _____
   _____
   _____

3. Ask God to reveal to you when you are being absent minded toward Him.

   _____
   _____
   _____
   _____

Focus On: Being Alone

> "No longer will they call you Deserted..."
>
> **Isaiah 62:4**

Why is it so easy to feel alone? From people not understanding to churches forgetting to be the Body of Christ, and a number of other reasons, loneliness is becoming more common; in the world and in the church. Often things such as loneliness are viewed, as weaknesses. The Body of Christ has become so focused on fitting the "perfect Christian" image that many tend to forget that His *"power is made perfect in weakness," (2 Corinthians 12:9)*. And beyond that, you were given Jesus as your high priest.

Hebrews 4:15 says, "For we do not have a high priest who is unable to sympathize with our weaknesses, but we have One who has been tempted in every way, just as we are – yet was without sin."

You serve a perfect God and were saved, by grace alone, through a perfect High Priest. Yet, you are not alone in your weaknesses in the flesh; even Jesus understands temptation. Through that, you can have hope that temptation does not need to seize you forever because Christ, fully God and fully man, was able to withstand temptation. Unlike Christ, you are not God, however, you do have the Holy Spirit dwelling within you, empowering you to resist temptation and strive for holiness.

"They will be called the Holy People, the Redeemed of the Lord; and you will be called Sought After, the City No Longer Deserted," (Isaiah 62:12).

Exposure to: Being Alone

1. When have you felt most alone?

   _____
   _____
   _____
   _____

2. How do you prevent temptation from seizing you?

   _____
   _____
   _____
   _____

3. Ask God to help you to strive for holiness.

   _____
   _____
   _____
   _____

Focus On: Your New Name

The world has so many names for you. When you were born, you were given a name, even one with meaning. As we grow up, new names were slowly added. From a caring parent, you may have received names like "Loved" or "Desired", while from a bullying peer, you may have received names such as "Unwanted" or "Forgotten".

"You will be called by a new name that the mouth of the Lord will bestow."

Isaiah 62:2

So often, the names the world tries to give you are not the ones your heart so desperately craves. You grow up believing lies about who you are, lies that are based on the opinions of others.

Yet there is hope! God chose you before the beginning of time. Your name is written in His book of life, and it is not a name of pain and brokenness but of love and kindness. The Lord desires for you to take hold of your new name, the one He has chosen for you. It is not the name your parents have given you, nor the one given by teachers or peers. Your new name is given to you by your Creator, who believes with His whole heart that you are who He determines you to be. This name for you, His name for you, cannot be taken away or marked by the words of this world, it is a name solely between you and the Lord.

"...To him who overcomes... I will give him a white stone with a new name written on it, known only to him who receives it," (Revelation 2:17).

Exposure to: Your New Name

1. What are some negative names the world has given to you?

   _____
   _____
   _____
   _____

2. Contrast those names with the truth of who the Word says you are.

   _____
   _____
   _____
   _____

3. Ask God to share with you what He calls you.

   _____
   _____
   _____
   _____

Focus On: Your Purpose

God created you with a purpose and a destiny. Before time began, He wrote out the plan of your life *(Psalm 139:16)*. He has proclaimed that, not only has He written out your life, but He also knows them. His plans for your life are to, *"give you hope and a future," (Jeremiah 29:11)*.

"For God's gifts and His call are irrevocable."

Romans 11:29

How great is it to know that your life has meaning? You are here for a purpose. It is easy to get caught up in the ways of this world and to feel as though there is no reason for life. That feeling is even found Biblically, like in the book of Ecclesiastes.

The amazing thing is, so much of the Bible reiterates God's plans for your life. And to truly know His plans is life changing. Since you are alive and breathing right now, God has a plan for you and your time on earth. Better still, His plans for you are good!

Ester 4:14 says, *"For if you remain silent at this time, relief and deliverance will arise for the Jews from another place and you and your father's house will perish. And who knows whether you have not attained royalty for such a time as this?"* God created you for a purpose. Maybe it does not make sense to you if you are going through a time of laying down your job or finances, but there is certainty in the fact that God made you for a reason. If you are in a season of struggle right now, do not give up, your, *"for such a time as this"* may bring freedom to others as well as to yourself.

"And we know that in all things God works for the good of those who love Him, who have been called according to His purpose," (Romans 8:28).

Exposure to: Your Purpose

1. What do you believe your purpose is?

   _____
   _____
   _____
   _____

2. Do you truly believe that God's plans for you are good? Why or why not?

   _____
   _____
   _____
   _____

3. Ask God how He is moving even in the struggles in your life, or ask Him where He was in a past season of trial.

   _____
   _____
   _____
   _____

Focus On: Being Known

"Oh Lord, You have searched me and You know me."

Psalm 139:1

A desire to be known is something set deep in the hearts of God's children. It is like being called out in a crowd, standing apart from those around you, being a unique and individual person.

Often times, this desire is found in the emptiness of the human heart, which you may try to fill the void by being known by the world. The appeal of fame and fortune goes far beyond the desire itself. The root of this desire is to be known and loved, but the way it often plays out is by seeking something God has not given you the favor to possess. Regardless of the reason for this searching, the deep-set desire is to be known.

There is hope in this desire to be known. How great it is to serve a God who knows you intimately and personally. It's the understanding of having someone who is known by the world to know you. Yet being known by God is greater than being known by any man on earth.

"...Your thoughts, O God! How vast is the sum of them! Were I to count them, they would outnumber the grains of sand..." (Psalm 139:17-18). These verses speak of God's thoughts toward you. If you were to calculate how often God thinks of you, based on an average lifespan of 80 years and the estimated number of grains of sand on the shores, God thinks positively of you 30 billion times a second.

He knows you intimately, desires you personally, want to connect with you in ways that we cannot understand. The desires of the Father's heart are to be in fellowship with His children. *"...You also may have fellowship with us. And our fellowship is with the Father and with His Son, Jesus Christ," (1 John 1:3).*

Exposure to: Being Known

1. Have you ever had the desire to be known by the famous or to be famous yourself? What was the root of that desire?

   _____
   _____
   _____
   _____

2. How does being known by God impact your life?

   _____
   _____
   _____
   _____

3. Ask God how He can fulfill that desire to be known in your heart.

   _____
   _____
   _____
   _____

Focus On: Being Remembered

"See, I have engraved you on the palms of my hands..."

Isaiah 49:16

There is a deep longing in the human soul to have meaning, to not be forgotten, to leave a legacy that exists beyond your life. You desire to be thought of in passing and checked up on by friends. And these are God given desires.

God created you with a need to be known, but not by the world, as is often assumed. He created you with a need to be known because He knows you deeply and intimately. In the Psalms it says, *"For You created my inmost being, you knit me together in my mother's womb," (Psalm 139:13)*. He knows you better than you know yourself because He created you and delights in the details of your life *(Psalm 37:23)*.

With so much going on in this world, it is easy to feel alone and forgotten. While people may fail you and keep to themselves, there is hope. God, your Heavenly Father and Creator, is thinking of you constantly. His thoughts are toward you and those thoughts are good. He looks into your heart and sees gold being purified through the flames. He looks to your face and sees beauty. Your sins are forgotten and covered by the blood of Jesus.

God cares about you. He cares about how you are doing and where you are in life. He desires to spend time with you, for you to let Him into the deep places of your heart. His heart is yours, always and forever.

"Though [a mother] may forget, I will not forget you!" (Isaiah 49:15).

Exposure to: Being Remembered

1. Recall a time when someone unexpectedly thought of you. How did that impact your life?

   _____
   _____
   _____
   _____

2. What does Isaiah 49:16 mean to you?

   _____
   _____
   _____
   _____

3. Ask God to speak to you how He remembers you each day. Record what He speaks below.

   _____
   _____
   _____
   _____

Focus On: Defying Criticism

You need to know God's truth in order to combat the lies of this world. In life, people may attempt to cause you to stumble. You will face criticism and rejection, opposition and setbacks.

> "Do not fret because of evil men..."
>
> **Psalm 37:1**

You cannot disprove lies without knowing the truth, and you cannot reject lies without believing the truth. The truth is God's Word, and you can overcome all obstacles through prayer. In Nehemiah, there was much opposition in rebuilding the walls of Jerusalem. At one point, Nehemiah wrote, *"They were all trying to frighten us, thinking, 'Their hands will get too weak for the work, and it will not be completed.' But I prayed, 'Now strengthen my hands,'"* (Nehemiah 6:9).

God had set a task before Jerusalem that was difficult but not impossible. Opposition was inevitable, yet they were not overtaken by it. When they were told they were too weak, Nehemiah prayed for strength. He knew that the source of his ability to complete any task was his strength through the Lord, so he relied on God to help him complete it.

When you face times of trial and opposition, you need to remember the Lord is by your side, never far away, and always as close as a prayer.

"They will call on My name, and I will answer them." (Zechariah 13:9).

Exposure to: Defying Criticism

1. When have you faced unwelcome criticism?

   _____
   _____
   _____
   _____

2. How did that criticism impact you?

   _____
   _____
   _____
   _____

3. Ask the Lord for a battle plan against attacks from anyone who may come up against you.

   _____
   _____
   _____
   _____

Focus On: Believing

It seems that negative words abound so prevalently in this world. Whether they come from parents or peers, the hearts of so many are plagued with disbelief. How you just need to hear words spoken over you that you are loved and cared for, that someone believes in you and will not leave you.

> "I have great confidence in you; I take great pride in you..."
>
> **2 Corinthians 7:4**

Your Heavenly Father is constantly speaking these words of life into your heart, Scripture is full of them. The meaning behind the stories of the Bible is His love, and the Word encompasses the love God has for you, His child.

Without having someone who is on your side, encouraging you to continue down difficult paths, it seems nearly impossible to continue walking through life. But you have the power of God compelling you to continue walking with Him, following His lead. While the world is shouting insults and criticism, the Spirit in you is whispering encouragement and support. You have the strength of the Lord to help you take each step. His words and guidance are a light to follow (*Psalm 119:105*).

Whenever the world is telling us you that you cannot complete the plans God has for you, God is standing for you and protecting you because, *"If God is for [you], who can be against [you]?" (Romans 8:31)*.

Exposure to: Believing

1. Record 3-5 reasons to believe God is for you.

   _____
   _____
   _____
   _____

2. Who do you have in your life that God has sent as a physical encouragement to you? How do they encourage you?

   _____
   _____
   _____
   _____

3. Ask God for a word of encouragement for you in this season of your life.

   _____
   _____
   _____
   _____

For more "Snapshot Encounters" check out Brianna's blog at:

http://BriPoster.com

To contact Brianna, email her at:

BriPoster@gmail.com